Fact Finders®

ENERGY REVOLUTION

GEOTHERMAL ENERGY

By M. M. Eboch

Consultant: Ellen Anderson
Executive Director of the Energy Transition Lab
Institute on the Environment
University of Minnesota, Twin Cities

CAPSTONE PRESS
a capstone imprint

Fact Finders Books are published by Capstone Press,
1710 Roe Crest Drive, North Mankato, Minnesota 56003
www.capstonepub.com

Library of Congress Cataloging-in-Publication Data
Names: Eboch, M. M., author.
Title: Geothermal energy / by M.M. Eboch.
Description: North Mankato, Minnesota : Fact Finders, an imprint of
   Capstone Press, [2019] | Series: Fact finders. Energy revolution | Includes
   bibliographical references and index. | Audience: Age 9. | Audience: Grades 4 to 6.
Identifiers: LCCN 2018040989 (print) | LCCN 2018042753 (ebook) |
ISBN 9781543555486 (eBook PDF) | ISBN 9781543555424 (library binding) |
ISBN 9781543559088 (pbk.)
Subjects: LCSH: Geothermal power plants—Juvenile literature. |
   Geothermal resources—Juvenile literature.
Classification: LCC TK1055 (ebook) | LCC TK1055 .E264 2019 (print) | DDC 333.8/8—dc23
LC record available at https://lccn.loc.gov/2018040989

Editorial Credits
Mandy Robbins, editor; Terri Poburka, designer; Jo Miller, media researcher;
Kathy McColley, production specialist

Photo Credits
Alamy: Joerg Boethling, 21; AP Images: Jeff Barnard, 4; Newscom: ZUMA Press/Guiziou
Franck, 11; Science Source: Claus Lunau, 22, Theodore Clutter, 25; Shutterstock:
anyalvanova, 29, Designua, 9, Dhimas Adi Satrina, 18, Ellen Bronstayn, 6, EpicStockMedia,
23, Gary Whitton, 14, jjspring, 10, MarcelClemens, 17, Mehmet Cetin, 27, Palmi
Gudmundsson, 12, Peter Gudella, Cover

Design Elements
Shutterstock: HAKKI ARSLAN, T.Sumaetho

Printed and bound in the USA
PA48

TABLE OF CONTENTS

CHAPTER 1

ENERGY UNDERGROUND

Klamath Falls, Oregon

Where does the electricity and heat in your home come from? Most of the energy people use now comes from fossil fuels. We burn gas, coal, and oil. But these forms of energy cause pollution, and they will eventually run out. What if you could heat your home with water from the ground instead? People do this in Klamath Falls, Oregon. The town uses wells that tap into underground water. This water is naturally hot. Hot water is piped under some roads and sidewalks. Its heat energy melts snow.

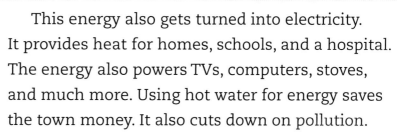

This energy also gets turned into electricity. It provides heat for homes, schools, and a hospital. The energy also powers TVs, computers, stoves, and much more. Using hot water for energy saves the town money. It also cuts down on pollution.

Heat from inside the earth is called **geothermal** energy. It is held in the rocks and water in the ground.

RENEWABLE ENERGY

More than 75 percent of the world's energy comes from fossil fuels. This percentage has been falling as people find alternatives. **Renewable** energy comes from nature. This may be heat from the sun or motion from the wind. It may be **hydropower** or geothermal energy. This energy is turned into electrical energy. Then people can use the energy just like they would if it came from fossil fuels.

geothermal—relating to the intense heat inside the earth

renewable—describes power from sources that you can use over and over again that cannot be used up, such as wind, water, and the sun

hydropower—a form of energy caused by flowing water

We know heat comes from the sun above us. But far below our feet, the earth is scorching hot as well. Just below the surface, the earth is cool. But the center of the earth is more than 10,000 degrees Fahrenheit (5,500 degrees Celsius). That's five times hotter than a campfire. It's as hot as the surface of the sun.

Layers of the Earth

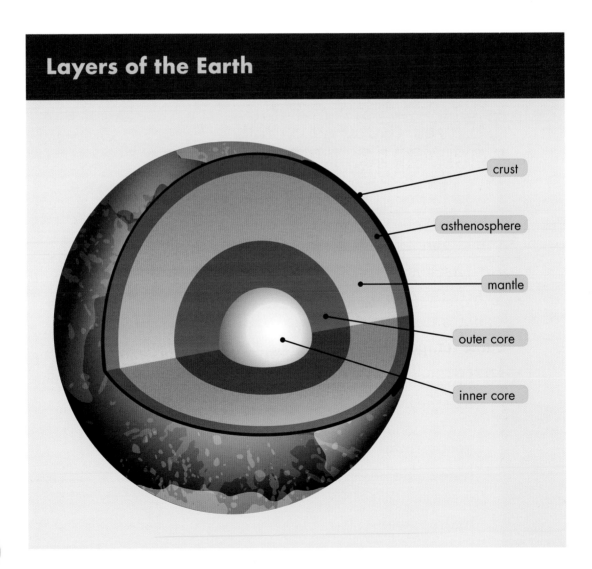

crust

asthenosphere

mantle

outer core

inner core

The hottest part of the earth is called the core. It is more than 3,000 miles (5,000 kilometers) underground. Heat from the core spreads outward. Each layer of the earth is cooler than the one below it. The top layer, the crust, is the coolest. But at the bottom of the crust, the temperature can reach 1,600°F (870°C). At this temperature, rocks begin to melt. The crust is warm enough there to provide energy people can use.

TEMPERATURE VERSUS HEAT

Temperature and heat are connected, but they are not the same. Temperature refers to how hot or cold something is. Heat itself is a form of energy. Heat depends on the size and type of the object. Temperature does not. Picture a large tub of hot water and a small cup of hot water. If they are at the same temperature, the tub has more heat. That's because the larger amount of water has the power to do more work, such as providing heat.

CHAPTER 2

HOW POWER PLANTS WORK

How does geothermal energy provide heat and electricity? Energy can change from one type to another.

A traditional power plant uses coal, natural gas, or oil. Workers burn these fuels to boil water. The boiling water turns into steam. As the steam moves through the air, it turns a large fan called a **turbine**. The fan's moving blades power a **generator**. This machine makes electricity by turning a magnet inside of a coil of wire. The magnets change the movement into electrical energy. The electricity is sent through wires into homes and businesses.

FACT

Fossil fuels come from plants or animals that died millions of years ago. Coal, oil, and natural gas are fossil fuels.

How a Geothermal Power Plant Works

Geothermal power plants start with hot water or steam from deep within the earth. The heat is converted to electricity. Then the water is returned back to the earth.

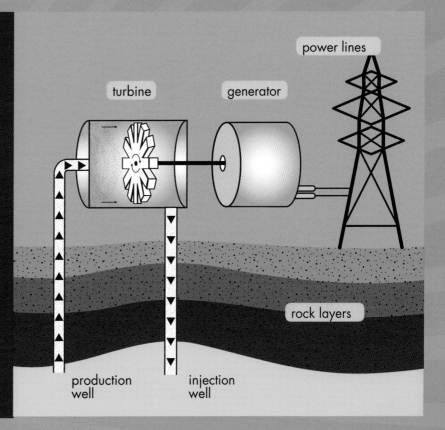

Geothermal power plants skip the first step. They don't burn fuel in order to heat water. Instead they use boiling water or steam from inside the earth. Pumps bring fluid from deep underground to the surface. Then these power plants make electricity the same way as traditional ones. Since they don't burn fossil fuels, they cut down on pollution.

turbine—a machine with blades that can be turned by a moving fluid such as steam or water

generator—a machine used to convert mechanical energy into electricity

USING THE EARTH'S HEAT

Geothermal power plants need two things—water and heat. The earth's crust is about 15 to 35 miles (24 to 56 km) thick on land. But in some places, the crust is thinner. In these cracks or channels, heat can rise toward the surface. Some places also have underground water. If the heat and water reach all the way to the surface, you may see hot springs. In these places it's easy to reach the earth's hot water.

Bathers enjoy the natural hot springs in the Atacama Desert in Bolivia.

People have visited hot springs since ancient times. They used the warm water for bathing, washing clothes, and cooking. In 1904 an Italian prince found another use for hot springs. He trapped steam coming from the ground in a valley called Val di Cecina and used it to turn a small engine. This made enough electricity to light five light bulbs. He proved that the earth's heat could make electricity. People in Italy built a power plant at that location in 1911. It was the first geothermal power plant in the world. Today that plant provides power to about 1 million homes.

The Larderello Val di Cecina geothermal plant uses Italy's natural hot springs.

ACCESSING GEOTHERMAL ENERGY

People in cities such as Klamath Falls, Oregon, can easily use the earth's hot water. Iceland has a lot of geothermal activity too. People there have used water from hot springs for bathing, cooking, and laundry for many years. Today about nine out of 10 homes in Iceland use geothermal energy for heat. They even heat swimming pools with it. In Iceland geothermal energy creates 25 percent of the country's electricity.

Not every country has hot springs. Those that do may have them only in a few places. Those places may be far from where people live. If people in places without hot springs want underground hot water, they have to dig for it. Geothermal power plants can be built in places without hot springs. They can work wherever the earth's crust is thin enough. Today companies can drill down 1 mile (1.6 km) or more to reach deep hot water or steam.

The Blue Lagoon is a natural hot spring in Iceland.

CHAPTER 3

GEOTHERMAL PROS AND CONS

Coal-fired power plants release harmful chemicals into the air.

Geothermal power plants have advantages over power plants that burn fossil fuels. Using fossil fuels to make power causes a lot of pollution. When fossil fuels are burned, they release chemicals. These chemicals make people sick and pollute lakes and rivers. They get into the air as greenhouse gases. The gases cause climate change, which causes rising sea levels and extreme weather. Geothermal power plants don't produce this pollution. They release 99 percent less carbon dioxide than fossil fuel power plants.

Geothermal energy is also renewable. These power plants remove hot water from the ground and use the heat. Then the water can be pumped back down into the ground. It picks up more heat so the same water can be used again and again. This means it will never run out.

Keeping Geothermal Energy Safe

In order to reach deep geothermal resources, rocks must be broken up. Some people worry that this could cause destructive earthquakes. It does cause tiny earthquakes far underground. But they are rarely felt on the surface. Scientists can measure these tiny quakes. This helps them understand what's happening underground. International guidelines make sure the rocks aren't cracked too far. Special machines report any problems before the cracks get too large.

OTHER RENEWABLE ENERGY SOURCES

Geothermal power is not the only type of renewable energy. Other sources include solar and wind power. All of these energy sources are cleaner for the environment than fossil fuels. But geothermal is better in some ways. Solar and wind energy depend on sun and wind. Solar power plants can't make energy at night. Wind energy doesn't work well when the wind isn't blowing. Geothermal power plants can work all day and night. They can work every day, no matter the weather. They also take up less land than solar and wind power stations do.

One disadvantage is that geothermal energy won't work everywhere. It will take several forms of renewable energy to replace the power that fossil fuels make today. Solar power works best in sunny areas. Wind power needs strong, steady winds. Geothermal power needs hot water from underground. Hydropower works best where there is a large amount of flowing water.

Wind turbines tower over solar panels. Both generate renewable forms of energy, like geothermal power.

CHAPTER 4

WHO USES GEOTHERMAL POWER?

The Dieng Valley in Indonesia is the site of a geothermal power plant.

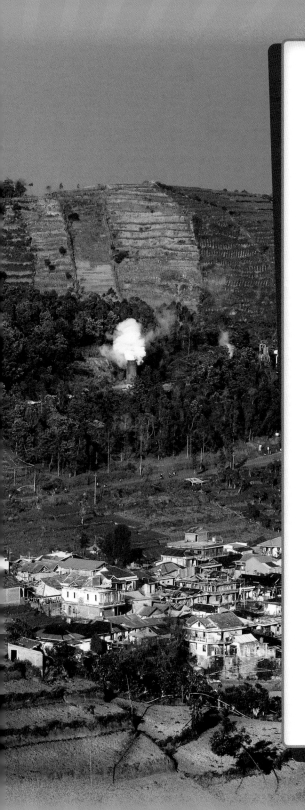

As of January 2016, 24 countries were using geothermal power. Today, those with the highest number of geothermal plants include the United States, the Philippines, Indonesia, and Mexico. Geothermal power is growing around the world. In 30 years, it could make up 10 to 20 percent of the world's energy. But right now, geothermal power is not widely used. It supplied less than 1 percent of the world's energy in 2015.

In the United States, some western states use geothermal energy. The earth's crust is thin or cracked in more places there. California produces the most geothermal energy. In other parts of the country, the earth's crust is too thick to easily access geothermal energy. It would be difficult and expensive to reach deep geothermal resources. Because of that, less than 1 percent of America's energy use comes from geothermal power. Even so, that's enough power for 3 million people.

FUNDING ALTERNATIVES

Most energy still comes from fossil fuels. You may wonder why, when renewable energy is better for the planet. Building new power plants costs a lot of money. It's easier and less expensive in the short term to keep using the old plants. But in the long term, it's a change that needs to happen for the good of all people and the planet.

Government support can help pay for new power plants. Many countries help fund both renewable energy and the fossil fuel industry. But right now fossil fuels get five times as much money as renewable energy. Giving more money toward developing renewable resources would reduce pollution and help fight climate change.

Government support can help solve other challenges too. The conditions needed for a geothermal power plant aren't common. Some areas are too cold or too dry. In other places the water can't move through the rock. Government funding could help companies design new systems. They might find ways to work around these challenges.

Building new power plants can cost billions of dollars. Government funding can help reduce those costs.

CHAPTER 5

LOOKING TO THE FUTURE

In geothermal district heating, cool water is sent to great depths. There it heats up. The rising steam is converted to energy. These systems may become more common in the future.

1000 meter

2000

3000

4000

5000

6000

What does the future hold for geothermal energy? New technology is being developed that could bring geothermal power to more areas. Some places have enough heat but not enough water. Or the water they have is trapped under solid rock. It's hard to drill down to that water. Enhanced geothermal systems could get to it. The systems shoot water into small cracks in the ground. This widens the cracks. Then water can move through the rock. As it rises, it gains heat from the warm rocks. The water becomes hot enough to make electricity.

RECYCLED WELLS

Old oil wells might be able to make new geothermal power. Thousands of oil wells are no longer used. They are deep enough to reach high temperatures underground. Scientists believe it's possible that water or steam pumped through these wells could be used to make power. This would be cheaper than drilling new wells.

Reusing old oil wells for geothermal power would be an environmentally friendly way to create new power.

OTHER OPTIONS

Some places may have water but not enough heat. Then lower-temperature systems can work. These **binary** cycle systems use groundwater that is less than 400°F (205°C). This fluid heats a second, or "binary," fluid in a heat exchanger. The second fluid boils at a much lower temperature than water. When it boils, the steam turns the blades in the turbine. These systems are also good for the planet. They put nothing into the air except water. About half of all current geothermal power plants use this system. There may be more in the future.

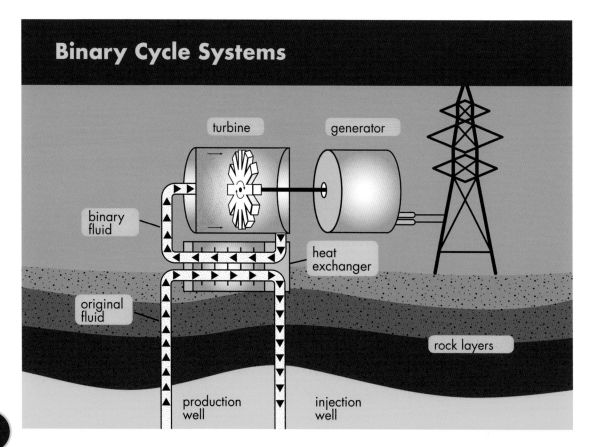

Binary Cycle Systems

turbine

generator

binary fluid

heat exchanger

original fluid

rock layers

production well

injection well

The future may also see more **cascading** geothermal projects. This process uses the same fluid several times. First, the fluid is used to make electricity. At this point the fluid is cooling but still warm. The system then provides heat and hot water. That can provide enough heat for certain uses. For example, the warm fluid could be used to keep greenhouses warm. It could also be pumped through pipes under sidewalks to melt snow.

binary—made up of two parts or units

cascade—to happen in a series where each step depends on the previous steps

Imperial Valley, California, is the site of a binary geothermal power plant.

GEOTHERMAL HEAT PUMP SYSTEMS

In some places, people can't reach hot underground water no matter what. Yet buildings can still use the earth's heat. Ten feet (3 meters) below the ground, the soil stays about the same temperature all the time. Throughout the year, that temperature is 45°F (7°C) to 75°F (21°C). That's often warmer than the air temperature in winter. In the summer, the ground is cooler than the air temperature.

A geothermal heat pump system makes use of the temperature difference between the air and the ground. Pipes containing fluid are buried underground. The fluid becomes the same temperature as the ground around the pipes. A pump exchanges heat between the earth and a building. In the winter, it pulls heat from underground to heat a building. In the summer, the pump can move heat from the building back into the ground. Geothermal heat pumps cost a little more to install than regular heating units. But they save 40 to 60 percent on heating and cooling costs each year. They are also the best heating and cooling systems for the environment. They release less than half the amount of greenhouse gases than other types.

A geothermal heat pump warms a shopping center.

FACT

The geothermal energy industry is growing fast. In the United States, 60,000 new geothermal heat pumps are installed each year.

GEOTHERMAL AND YOU

Does working with geothermal energy sound interesting to you? You may want to study engineering. An engineer is someone who designs and builds machines. Geothermal power plants employ many **engineers**.

The geothermal industry also needs scientists. Geothermal resources are not always easy to find. Geologists are scientists who study the earth. They can help figure out what's happening underground. Chemists are scientists who can help find geothermal resources by studying the chemicals in well water.

What will the future bring? Geothermal energy could provide much more power to the United States than it does now. Many countries could get all of their power from geothermal energy. But for that, we'll need better systems. That requires people with creativity who can solve problems.

People who work with geothermal power help keep our world running. They do it in a way that is kind to our planet. Could you be one of those people?

....

engineer—a person who uses science and math to plan, design, or build

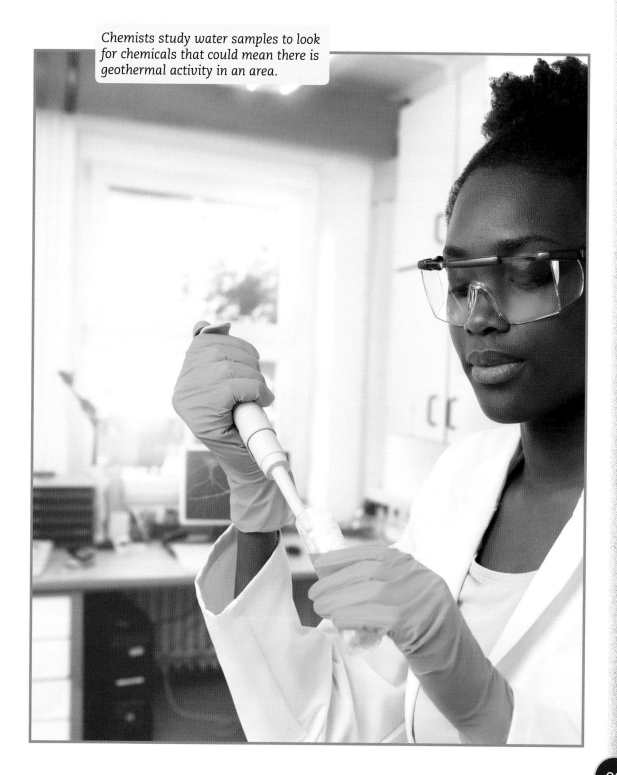

Chemists study water samples to look for chemicals that could mean there is geothermal activity in an area.

GLOSSARY

ancient (AYN-shunt)—from a long time ago

binary (BYE-nuh-ree)—made up of two parts or units

cascade (kass-KADE)—to happen in a series where each step depends on the previous steps

climate change (KLY-muht CHAYNJ)—a significant change in Earth's climate over a period of time

engineer (en-juh-NEER)—a person who uses science and math to plan, design, or build

generator (JEN-uh-ray-tur)—a machine used to convert mechanical energy into electricity

geothermal (jee-oh-THUR-muhl)—relating to the intense heat inside the earth

hydropower (HYE-droh POU-ur)—a form of energy caused by flowing water

renewable (ri-NOO-uh-buhl)—power from sources that will not be used up, such as wind, water, and the sun

turbine (TUR-bine)—a machine with blades that can be turned by a moving fluid such as steam or water

READ MORE

Bard, Mariel E. *Geothermal Energy: Harnessing the Power of Earth's Heat.* Powered Up! A STEM Approach to Energy Sources. New York: PowerKids Press, 2018.

Grady, Colin. *Geothermal Energy.* Saving the Planet Through Green Energy. New York: Enslow Publishing, 2017.

Mangor, Jodie. *Geothermal Energy.* Alternative Energy. Minneapolis: Core Library, an imprint of Abdo Publishing, 2017.

INTERNET SITES

Use FactHound to find Internet sites related to this book.

Visit www.facthound.com

Just type in 9781543555424 and go.

 Check out projects, games and lots more at **www.capstonekids.com**

CRITICAL THINKING QUESTIONS

1. Do you think geothermal power would work well where you live? Why or why not?

2. Many different fields of science are involved in the geothermal industry. Which is more interesting to you—engineering, chemistry, or geology? Why?

3. Geothermal power does not work well everywhere. New technology could bring it to more areas. Should we support new geothermal technology? Or should time and money go to different forms of energy? Why?

INDEX